Eightfold:
Navigating QTPOC intersections
Eli Ryn Brown

Published by **Lost Alphabet**

With offices at:
1603 Capitol Ave. Cheyenne, WY 82001

United States of America www.lostalphabet.com

ISBN-10: 099856026X
ISBN-13: 978-0998560267

Library of Congress Cataloging in Publication data available upon request.

Printed in the United States of America

TABLE OF CONTENTS

To those queer and trans people of color who
have known the same lows as I:
May you find balance.

It is hard to stop lying to yourself, rather, myself. It's hard to accept responsibility, to claim. I try to explore the four noble truths. How do we escape suffering? Through understanding? By embodying truth? It is still hard for me to be honest with myself at all times. I used to lie out of a deep desperation. I would pretend to not see the truth inside, in front. But it sept out with each act of defiance towards school, parents, and my own body. I was trying to silence myself, to give people distractions. My reflection was a bathroom mirror completely fogged. These days I'm trying to be true. I am trying to accept myself, to see all of myself unfiltered, and balance that with my projected image. To eventually stop even projecting an image, and just live. But that is far away. For now, I will taste suffering like the after taste of candy on my tongue. It lingers persistently but my body slowly washes it away.

Black Don't Crack

They say black don't crack. My grandmother's skin
is still smooth at 72. Sometimes I look at my
mixed skin and wonder if it will look the same.

They say black don't crack. Does that apply to the
youth I see? Their skulls seem to crack under
baton and boot every time a cop deems it lawful.
Thugs ought to be killed, surely. 95-cent cigars are
the cost of a life. Toy guns must look more
realistic in brown hands.

They say black don't crack. The whip sound is
resonant even if slavery is over. The systematic
oppression designed by our forefathers still snaps
necks and sends bullets through the unarmed
backs of dark, smooth skinned children. Post-
racial America is truly a blessing.

My black cracks with every slain sibling of skin
and I feel the guilt of my lightness. I am half
oppressor and half oppressed fighting for
dominance in a wrinkle free space of privilege. If
my voice is heard I speak for the dead as their skin

darkens and cracks in their coffins.

Image

You said I was a demon, and so I became one. My tongue did not fork; my feet were not cloven. Rather I became a reflection of a negative image. I came to occupy only negative space.

You said I was a demon, and so I learned to lie. I thieved and manipulated. I hated, how I hated! All I saw and could be was tainted. Each day was a calculated step into oblivion.

This demonic negative space! How can I be in this translucent black and white still shot? There is color to be filled. I know there must be.

You said I was a demon, and so of course I was! Underbelly skin scaled, I slide in and out of this world.

There is Renaissance in Every Revolution

WeHo Jazz bar,

why can't I see my reflection in your hues and

haze?

I hear it in the trumpet that swirls historic notes,

smooth and heavy on my eardrums.

I see it in the wall frames.

Elongated black bearded face – what did they do

to your authenticity?

How did you lose your history, Jazz bar?

Am I representing you on this stool, commanding

attention?

Or am I simply searching for unscathed mirrors in

a city of shattered glass?

I will sigh melanin dipped poetry into your

nostrils, Jazz bar, and

we will inhale together,

revived.

THOUGHT

I am often torn between states of attachment and detachment. It is hard to find the balance. I used to detach from even myself. Floating through days code switching, gender introspection far from my mind but deep in my belly always. I would watch my body from a far, seeing the path it was going on and trying to slow it down, throwing obstacles in its way. Drugs, infatuation, late nights in the cold air with people twice my age. Always on the brink of life or death, or worse yet, neither. An overwhelming moment of hesitation stretched for years. A continual gasp for air as I broke myself down. I did it for so long, for fear had paralyzed me. I clung to everything, attached to the familiarity even if it was painful. Detached from the real me for the convenient me. The socially acceptable me. I had no truth until I was stripped bare of all possible guises. I fought myself to the death and was breathed into life instead.

Gold Coast, Chicago

People looked at me with fear

in their eyes today

on the street, pedestrian

aggression, sidewalk side eye.

I exist in their view,
enraging them with inhabited space.

My quiet revolution:

sit comfortable in my skin,
ball my fist - raise it high.

My Body is Disruptive

Not disruptive, in the way that a raised portion of
sidewalk might grip at your shoe, but in the way
that blood leaks from ovaries without warning
leaving stains like old nosebleeds on concrete. I
hid my first period.

I am not made of bricks, but of the pillow cases
in street alleys that are lined on the inside with red
crumbly dust and decorated on the outside with
soiled fingerprints, and displaced hair.

The soft edges of my hipbones are my
metropolitan, minimalist cityscape. Structuring
iron rods that will never bend with a fetus. If I
focus only on my hipbones and the way they 45-
degree-angle at my femurs then maybe I might
forget the fissures in between. Assigned female at
birth.

I don't ignore them because I am uncomfortable,
but because of the unsettled minds of those

around me who have never even really looked at me. Somehow this opening of anatomy gave me bloodline responsibility. The day I came out my mother planted her stillborn daughter image of me in my belly.

I am pregnant with parental loss and my neonatal supplements have been replaced with biweekly injections, testosterone has momentarily dried my tears. I have not bled this month.

My body is disruptive in the way that hormones can halt past puberty. In the way that double incisions can sledgehammer chest formations. In the way that others pause with my pronouns. In the way my presentation has caused the death of a female child. In the way I birthed myself at 21 from the coffin I was raised in.

Disruptive, but for not me, not anymore.

Blended

Yellow paint on my shins,
drying in my leg hair.
Brightening the scabs on my knuckles.

Blue paint on your collar bone,
lightly trailing down your spine.
Around the freckle behind your ear.

Green paint on
my chest, the tips
of your
fingers. The
corners of our
mouths.

SPEECH

I am known as a talkative person to most. Speech
can have a way of magic about it. How you say
what you say, and when you say - it can all serve as
acts of creation, destruction. Words weave images
of memory to be passed from mind to mind, or
projections of futures to be shared. I used to rely
heavily on words as a vanishing act. Choose the
right group of words and poof – there goes my
"blackness." Or I found myself whispering my
blackness into familiar ears. Utter the right slang
and there too creeps in the hint of queerness.
Constructing a constant series of ever changing
character maps to those around me, I lived behind
a matrix of words that catered vulnerability in
small doses. I told small truths while holding back
fear-inducing ones. My bond with words is just as
deep as my freedom from them. As soon as I
could transform my whispered truths into shouts

of pride, until I could say my name in all spheres,
I was burying myself in half-meant exposition.
Both cyclical and backwards in momentum. But
when I embraced truth in all words, or at least
strove towards it, I was released from it in the
same breath. Words communicate the depths of
our being, but they are always a layer removed
from purity. Therein lies poetry. The hand may be
dirty and it may be mangled, but still the grasping
of those weathered fingertips at true expression is
in all regards poetry.

A Letter to the Young Black Activist

They never taught me about the black women that sent white men to space. They never told me about the black trans women who led and bled for the lgbtq community. They never told me about the black men that died in greatness so that others could claim their glory. They told us our history started with slavery so that we forgot about the long thriving roots we held in Africa. I will tell my children. I will teach the students. I will make their paths known.

This revolution is not new; this experience is not an anomaly. Every darker child in American history from the generations before us has felt the creeping noose of discrimination at their clavicle. Many died in the tree before ever taking an unrestricted breath.

I am thankful to the grandparents of the non-white millennial for laying Jim Crow shields around their offspring and teaching the downward

gaze that sometimes minimized the brutality, but
the time has come to shout as loud as their silence.

The elderly should not have to finish what
America halted. Pick up your pen, open your
laptop, shout at the march and bear your souls at
the foot of every courthouse in the nation. This
revolution will not come without sacrifice and
community action plans will not glide over
morning toast like margarine.
It will be molasses, dark and slow spilling into our
glands. Our pores may clog but sweat will push
through and we can become one with the message
before it is one with the people. We must carry
this sweetness just as we do our melanin, we must
hold our dirtied hands and bind together.
Tomorrow is too late a promise for action.
Mobilize the movement.

Transgender, Translanguage

Every word I write drives me further from the truth of my identity. Each attempt at accurate language is a wedge between my explanation and my expression. The words that we are taught are catered and cultivated towards the binary and leave those in between or outside gasping in silence. How can you tell me language is inclusive?

Gender is like the color spectrum. Humans can see a set spectrum of colors and only have the vocabulary to describe these few. Empirically, we know there are more which other species can see but because of the lack of language and the static nature of heteronormativity, which might I add glares back to me in Microsoft word while underlined in red, we struggle to communicate our identities. Our colors are refuted as we search dictionaries for kind-of-sort-of definitions. Oxford and Webster have not yet validated my existence.

So I sit at the page each night mute speaking to
the blind and deaf with borrowed and inapplicable
words. I grasp at letters and sounds hoping their
combinations will somehow illuminate the
possibilities of my queerness in a country where
the president simply saying LGBT for the first
time in a state of the union address is supposed to
scream progress.

I sit at tables with my parents sweating and
sobbing trying to stutter out an explanation of
why the daughter they thought they had never
existed but no, not a son either, I don't know,
closer to son than daughter if I use the terms you
know but fuck you because that's not how it
works and I'm sorry because there is no way for
you to know any better. They don't teach this in
schools or write about it in parenting books. I can
barely finish this thought in my head let alone try
and tell you how to relearn every textbook and
science class you ever read or took.

Having the words man and woman hug your skin
at night silently and without qualm is something I

want you to appreciate as I explain that the pronoun they can be singular with every introduction. Never pausing during the check M or F or please write your full name is something I hope you cherish because I once spent an hour staring at two empty boxes in a waiting room knowing either was a lie and sweating at the thought of a triggering birth name.

If language serves your identity instead of obliterating it, if you can pick up any book or turn on the TV and see anything even close to representation take a step back and listen to us as we tell you something more exists, that we exist. We give words to entities that we deem worthy of recognition. I beg you, be patient as I search for mine.

Tokens

I find it ironic
that the place I chose to read a book on black
power
and Buddhism
RADICAL DHARMA

I am confronted with a table
thin, white-skinned,
possibly Mexican,

'nigga
nigga
NIGGA
I grew up in the hood, my nigga
this shit aint the same when I say it'

because a nigga is poor
because a nigga is from the hood -
he tells his white friends

'nigga if you had a gold chain
maybe you could get like me'

because a nigga is chains
and a fuckboy fade
a nigga is a costume

and I am torn between
theory and practice

is the root of my discomfort
in his language
or in the whiteness that surrounds him

I, too, have performed

CONDUCT

I have always struggled with how to act. There
have been times when I surrounded myself with
people who acted in ways that hurt others. There
have been times when I hurt others. Be it through
drugs, lies or the inescapable mix of the two, my
past is not to be looked at through solely my own
pain. There was always the pain of others at my
hand. It is often difficult to act without grounding
yourself first in a reality. And since I lived in so
many altered states, there was no basis or
limitations to how far I would go to keep them all
circulating, keep the distractions going,
simultaneously. Now I try to have a balanced code
of conduct. One that is not so rigid or shifting,
but emanates from within. I have found my
systems of humility and light and I was liberated

from the pain I caused. I think in many cases we act out of fear and desperation. It makes us feel blameless to our conduct. But this is not the case. There is still the hurt left behind. Each step toward lovingkindness I take today is an act of balancing. I hope to act out of love instead, without the trail of broken hearts, without the constant personal heartbreak.

Mind Over Matter

There's a new trend in pseudo intellectual circles
to talk about how poetic cell replacement is. That
the body replaces its cells every 7 years and it is
new and clean and untouched. They are rejoicing
at the fact that the ominous "you" loses impact
over time and the strength of human body has
preserved itself once again.

I can't see how this promise of fresh skin lightens
their minds because it's been 9 years and I still feel
jagged fingernails piercing my thighs and the
sharpness of whiskey sweat in my nostrils.

My body could replace itself ten times over and I
would still hear the sound my nail made as it tore
from my finger and lodged itself in the wall. A
new one has grown but it still aches at the thought
of clawing. The freshness of my adult hands does
not stop their shaking.

I spent years of my youth opening my flesh and creating my own barriers in scar tissue, my forearm an abandoned prison tally. Every heaving breath I took in locked bathrooms behind shower curtains was dank and sour with iron.

There's a new collection of cells in my body that aren't supposed to be the same as the ones you pillaged all those years ago. They were formed in fire and I walk constantly on coals because even with the romanticized science of body my brain matter remains the same ravaged collection of an 11-year-old bleeding in a tub.

First Attempts

I keep letting people try and feel things through
me – love, safety, acceptance. I am a walking
emotional safe spot and this makes all the fellow
sad and confused twenty something's in my life
think that maybe my comfort is good for them.
Maybe I will nurture them into happiness.

But I can't. And I see it from the start. I know the
patterns and watch myself fall into false
domesticity. I spend weeks coming home with
songs and poems and wildflowers of half-truths. I
hold people through the night until they kiss me
through their tears.

We lay sweating and breathing each other in at
4ams, as we don't talk about why we feel so sad
after sex. We let our chests heave into each other's,
melting healthy friendship boundaries with each
absentminded-trailing fingertip. In the moment
the connection is addictive, bodies intertwined and

names moaned, we mainline body fluid and stay
high on our ability to find intimacy in the napes of
necks.

Knowing all of someone's details can feel so
damn poetic that we force the romance into it
even though we know ours is not that kind of
poem. It's one of fragments and broken stanzas
and chaotic order and

ultimately they break down. They cry and say
sorry and tell me to stop being so kind to them,
stop comforting them. If I stop I'll have to look at
myself, feel for myself. And so I hold them, let
them kiss me through their tears, and assure them
that love will come, just not with me.

I knew it was never going to be me. Not like this,
not while we push our collective sadness between
us and run with it above our heads, arms shaking
under the weight. But I can pretend it might be
me for the downward spiral, the exhilaration of
the last effort before collapsed elbows, until we
plunge back into ourselves.

Creeping Vines

Your limbs vine around my skin and I let the sap
of our sweat bind us.
    Every night you wrap farther around me,
timidity falling off with routine.
        I breathe in your carbon dioxide and
mark time with your heart beating against my
stomach.
            I spend 4ams pretending to be
asleep, your steady wall to lie on.
                When your hands shift I
            feel them on my skeleton.
                    When I am bold
                I slide my own under
                yours for you to grip.
            But last night, my fingertips
        started to grow their own vines.
        Your hips had rocked back into mine, a
complete seal of skin.
And I interlaced my hands in yours.

You rolled on your back to
untangle for a moment.

I slid under your
arm and placed my head
on your chest.

Never had you held me, let me
stick myself to you.

No, never had I let my vines expand, and
interlace with yours.

My heart was counting seconds too fast.

But you, more awake
than I thought, put me to sleep with trailing leaf
fingers.

Up and down my back, to match
the small smile on your mouth.

We sleep in slow
motion.

We are vined in
vulnerability.

LIVELIHOOD

It took me a while to figure out any possibilities for jobs that would make me happy. My dreams of making it big in the literary world were dashed by my constant fear induced paralyses. How could I ever write anything with an ounce of authenticity on the grand scale while hiding who I was? Sure, I could produce endless poetry and stories for those at my college or in my personal friend group. The near and dear queers and classmates. But I rarely submitted material to any publication that could start a career. And my work was constantly in a state of "almost". Maybe it still is. But before I came out every piece I wrote felt as if I was holding something back. Putting emphasis on a false climax in the plot. Omitting. This is not to say anything or pass judgements on "the closet." But lying to yourself is different than not coming out. A deeper symptom maybe, a coping method to say the least. Anyhow, I was aimless for a while. And after wandering and seeking, I started to tell myself the truth more days than not. I chose exposure over fear and it no longer mattered where my path took me because how I lived was free. Bestsellers or not. The reason I had wanted to be read by others, to sell and write books, was just to share some light with those out there living in similar shadows, paralyzed. To say I had been there too, and still darkened by them at times. To let it go. I can do that in other ways, though. Work to help, and help to love are my only requirements now. And I feel myself accepting better opportunities somehow. In all regards, learning the variety of charity and community work one can do has renewed and cleansed my spirit even as some around me contest my peace.

If you can reverse a narrative,
Can you reverse reality?

Police Report:

White cop approximately 6 feet tall

Two accomplices, gang of personnel to follow

Gun holder – grazed by thumbs continually

Possible offenses – resisting release of hostages,

One-hour detainment of 4 individuals in their

early 20s,

Has not confessed to motive

Suspected racial tension

Entered residence without warrant

Hostage statements lost

No charges pressed.

As I Came to Boil

There are flames beneath my feet
Licking my soles,
I am past the simmer.
These late nights have been plagued with
projection,
Why is it when I say 1 others hear 5?

It's too much, it's too much
I want to love on my own terms.
The rapid

click - gas - fire

Of my surroundings is bubbling within me.
At the foreground I am lost romantically and in
the giant backdrop of 2017 I am consistently
burnt by the political.

I shed your anger as I shed your latency issues
with trust

(this could have been easier, this could have been
easier, I am not the one who gave up).

I shed my expression for the night and let the heat
transform me (I am not my country, but I can
expose its tenderness).

I've been circulating in this boil, pressurized and
sweating but my soul has been cleansed and my
heart sings not today,

not today.

45

Last night my country looked me dead in the eye

and told me I am unimportant.

Over its shoulder at the polls tellin me my life

don't matter.

America I love you and you've given me all I have.

But when white America keeps turning its back on

blacks

when rich America keeps looking away from the

poor,

when straight America decides that the VP, a

champion of conversion therapy,

is the right choice for more than just the right

wing

it fills me anger my bones shake in fear.

Knowing everything I hold dear

could slip through the cracks of this political

sideshow,

this corporate democracy.

A young black lawyer, my brother, spoke

about our choices

privatized candidates that push people to

extremes.

We've abandoned the local, the people, the cause.

So now we stand a nation divided half of us

needin emotional gauze.

The state of the union can't begin to be

addressed.

50% of white women voted for a rapist.

I understand it takes time to un-internalize

misogyny,

unlearn patriarchy and redefine your morality.

But I had faith in the people the surrounded me.

My own cousin decided his love for me was not

enough,

rather he decided he was the one who should be

put above

all others around him. Saying lazy immigrants have

no jobs

while he lives in the house his parents pay for.

This country has me shook for my people.

We're long past the charade of living in a land of

equals,

but I refuse to let the fear silence my voice.

I fear for my rights but I still have a choice
to stand up and be loud, I will never again feel
small.
I still believe in America, its potential despite its
weakness.
I am humbled by her wrath but equal to her
graces.
As are you, and every one of us if we stay active
as we can.
Uplift your sister and your neighbor every
minority
The country has growing pains and we the joints
bear the brunt
Turn that rage into love, take the pain and make it
meaningful.
My black, trans, and queer existence is my
resistance.
Linguistic weaponry an arsenal I utilize with my
privilege.
I promise each and every one of you there is
power to be shared.
Its contingent on our perseverance, show the
world we care.

ENDEAVOR

To try at all is in itself a feat. I spent a long period of time being afraid to put effort into myself, my studies, my ambitions. It seemed that each effort to push myself involved a level of exposure and vulnerability that I was extremely uncomfortable with. I could not bear the chance of people discovering how fragmented the portrayal of myself I had presented them with had become. As a child, before puberty, if I liked it I went for it. If I had to move up a grade to be challenged, into strange classrooms I went. I even went to read with the older kids instead of napping in kindergarten. There was no fear of spotlight or attention. This was before I had learned there could be an acceptable or unacceptable anything. Besides simple playground and household rules, I was living as authentically as possible. It was a beautiful gift. But as I began to grow up more I had interactions with societal norms and guidelines. I found I was going to encounter a great deal of resistance. First, in the realm of sexuality, I was spending my time mostly crushing on girls. This was an instant source of contention between myself, my peers and parents. This was the beginning of my education in lies, in drugs, in portrayal of self and in escapism I lost the meaning of truth. I also became more and more confused about my gender identity. What I saw in the media were these demonized instances of trans people and stereotypical depictions of butch lesbians. And so from that ever present fear instinct of self-preservation, I came out as gay instead of touching the gender topic. That did not seem an available option. I did not want to be killed. So many reflections of my possibilities and intersections seemed to end in untimely and violent death.

Brown Earth Skin

Quiet me. Fill my mouth with cotton and watch
my fingers bleed with history.

Birth me in a noose, best hung from low hanging
branches from the tree of life. Be patient as I
marinate in internalization.

Touch me. Do not be perverse. Touch behind my
ears and knees; catch the salt tap beneath my lids.

Lay me down and pepper my ears, salt my lips,
pour lemon juice in the seams of my skin.

Peel away this oppressive body, politically
tenderized flesh. Set my melanin rind out to dry.

Lie beside my chilled marrow and find shade in
this garden bed of my fingernails.

Fillet my muscles and turn my fat to grease. Lick
clean my bones, leave nothing but lightly
complected calcium and bury the rest.

Thigh Cramp

Sometimes the difficulties that can come with
being trans are hard to explain.

Not why they are difficult because most
understand the violence is distressing, the
ignorance is rampant, the internal conflict is high.

But how they are difficult.

How it feels to stare at your thigh for an hour on a
Monday night, your dominant hand holding a long
sought after boost to your sense of self, paralyzed
even though it's everything you want because it's
still an inch and a half long needle that has to
puncture intramuscularly into your flesh and you
have to try not to think of why you need it in the
first place.

How it feels to have a span of time longer than
usual where you're feeling low dysphoria and then
a stranger misgenders you at work, school, on the

street, your lungs seem to shrivel as you find a
reply that doesn't betray how your heart has
seemed to stop beating.

How it feels when you wish you could invite your
friends or loved one to a family party but you feel
anxiety creep up your spine knowing that your
birth name will be thrown around loosely by all
and the need to apologize to your guest for silent
and unknowing attacks is something you can't
muster the energy for.

It's easy to understand why daily trials and
constant obstacles are prevalent for trans people if
you're anyone with an ounce of compassion, but I
wish I could explain how there are sandbags tied
around my ankles filled with microaggressions and
shame and I do love myself but the rope is
rubbing me raw and my thighs are

just so tired.

Reduce, Reuse

There's a new green flowering in the bruise on my
hipbone, extending its fingers towards the depths
of purple and yellow almost desperately reaching
out.

I take my thumb and press into it, fingernail first.
They're jagged from biting and start to sink in,
adding a deep red to the palate. There are little
bubbles of molten scab crusting, volcanic rock
under my skin.

I keep pushing until I'm knuckle deep, if I can get
my whole hand in maybe I'll reach my ovaries and
plunge into its surface. Does it feel like a heart or
more like a brain? I'll take each defective egg and
serve them at dinner like caviar to everyone who
knows me. Proper mourning procedures for half
deaths and hormonal redistribution.
I'll reach past and emerge from my belly button
inside out. Flip my whole body until just my ring

finger is stuck inside then sever it like an umbilical cord.

It's not rebirth just recycled parts.

MINDFULNESS

Are you aware of your surroundings? When I was
14 I sat watching an Aikido examination and
thought - he never sees the attack until it surprises
him. I sat there, scrutinizing his movements and
the faults I perceived in them. Too clunky,
mechanical. Always searching for the attacker
instead of occupying his space and flowing the
attacker out of it. I examined him for maybe 5
minutes as the test went on. A viewer stood from
the benches behind me, off the mat, and walked
towards the bathroom. She bumped my back and
I jumped, taken off guard, mind shaken. When I
returned my gaze to the exam, I realized there was
a reason I was at the back of the mat, and not
with the instructors on the testing board. It would
be years before I sat on the other side, but I had
learned a lesson that day that I never forgot, and
took with me through the ranks. I am not always
aware. I have not perfected mindfulness, because
it must be constant. Of course, after being
humbled I pledged silently that I would always be

aware from that point on. That too, was a naïve
mistake, which I would learn soon enough.
Mindfulness, in its complete form, expands form
within and exists in peace. Not peace in the
positively connoted way, as nice a thought that is.
Peace in the sense of neutrality, in stillness. The
body may run and attackers may come, the world
could be ablaze or quicksand at your feet, but the
mind must remain still. Aware of all around it,
sensing the atmosphere. I have slowly gained the
ability to be mindful, to be still, but I have not
reached constancy. I no longer judge this.

To Be and not to be

I am Hamlet and Ophelia and
        the apparition.
I am immobile in fear and unstable in life and
transparent,
        paper thin.
I am desire when you look, I am shame when you
turn, every action with my eyes fixed on
        where we have been.

I am between your finger tips and beneath your
heels, I am bullshit and self-indulgence. I am the
fictionalized truth, and truthful fiction carved
quietly
        into our skin.

I am stuck and I can't stop.
I am contradiction.

15 Times, She

We introduced each other in class today and 15
times, she, only one Eli.
I sat with my head bowed and all of my activist
voice shrank inside me with each she that pressed
on my chest as tight as my binder.

15 times I flinched and sat in the confusion of
those around me, all eyes swimming with
pronouns.

I adjusted my shirt in the way of so many trans
boys, obscuring my chest, so their eyes moved to
my arms and jaw.

I tried not to flex and reinforce their
preconceptions.
At moments like this my fingers twitch as if they
could reach into each dictionary and remove all

beginning S's from the collective vocabulary.
Maybe this would keep me from also wanting to
slip from my skin.

15 times, she, and 15 mental whispers from my
cowardice, he.

Timing

When I first encountered the small of your back,
my hands guiding you into a room,
I was overwhelmed by a lifetime of open doors.

I apologize for closing some,
fear is an instinct I have not yet tamed.

But I'm growing.

Through the window I see a path,
drizzled in moonlight,
calling out.

I pray the soles of our feet
meet the soil in unison.

MEDITATION

I cannot teach you to meditate. I cannot claim to
know how, completely, either. Not to say I haven't
had wonderful instruction. It's come to me in
many ways – from martial, spiritual and
therapeutic teachers. I've dipped the soles of my
feet into it all. But I did not fully submerge myself
until I realized they were all the same, and none of
them existed. The ways of learning are numerous
because we are numerous, and all receive and learn
in different manners. But the meditation is the
same. The breath: find your way to its depths and

make it pure. Cleanse the mind. Discipline your entire being, become both empty and full. Meditation taught me that nothing is real, and yet we are all anchored in some view of reality. We let these realities dictate our actions and feelings, and again meditation washes it all away. It is breath in its simplicity. It is life.

Breaking Form

I need to
                              breathe out

I just keep sucking in air this breeze feels nice
but my
lungs can't keep up I'm so
                              inflated

on this mountain side more of a hillside really as
fox tails
dig into my heels I lent someone my shoes at the
top and
they

                              ran

I couldn't chase them with all this air so I floated a
bit
and sat down on a rock formation I was in
between
boulders and I just

                                        melted

into its cracks and now I'm stone – dusted, flaking
and the
air seeps out past my chapped lips I still have my
shirt
you don't need shoes with limestone toes I should
stop
giving my clothes to everyone I meet it's so hard
being
naked

                                               out
                                        I'm breathing
                                               out
and I have to break form it's time to breath,

                                            in.

. - - .

drain - incision - incision - drain

I shave my head, transform, refresh

I throw a look, I claw out of this funk

drain - incision - incision - drain
This pattern on my chest is
staccato scars, meaningless Morse
they are neither on or off display

drain - incision - incision - drain
my expression is sloppy

but true

Becoming

The law and order of the cosmos does not pause
to speak to me,
rather I pause to feel its presence more accurately

Dharma name, rising

I am surrounded by a mental forest of bamboo in
a hurricane
sleek brown poles of malleable strength,
they keep structure in all directions

Dharma name, clearing

They are the same as the staff
that brings my mind to clarity with each strike and
humility to my body with each misstep,
reverberating in my palms with a sincerity of form
I try to soak into my ki, and extend out of my
being.

I straighten my spine with breath,

Dharma name: bamboo.

ACKNOWLEDGEMENTS

I am so honored to be able to have my first little
collection floating out in the universe. Thank you
to all those at Lost Alphabet who made that
possible. I'm so glad I entered your contest.
I would not be here and who I am if it weren't for
my parents, and brother. You've put up with a lot
of wild, and I'm glad we're as close as we are now.
Gaby – you've always been patient and kind with
everything I've written. You were my first poetic
encouragement.
My second source of encouragement after I
started writing poetry I found at UCR (#D329). I
appreciate all the buds, like Ash and Ro and so
many others, who listened to every draft with
understanding and oh so queer ears. Also to all my
professors and TAs with their continual pushing
of my boundaries and open ears, thank you.
Special shout out to Rachelle Cruz and Susan
Straight for being inspiring professors. Also, to
Lindsey Steffes for letting me spill my guts via
poetry in office hours every week for an entire
quarter. I went through a healing that I will not
forget.
To my longest friend, Nicolas, thanks for truly
being down for whatever my life has thrown our
way. You are the embodiment of loyalty.
A big internet thanks to the AmbuguiT Guys and
all who have contributed to the trans and GNC
youtube community. I came out on the internet far
before anywhere else. So many of you are family
to me.

Last, but certainly not least, thank you to my
second family at OC Aikido, for keeping me alive
and teaching me the discipline and calm I was not
ready to learn from my own parents.

To all my friends and family, I love you. Thank
you for supporting me.
To my LGBTQIA+ siblings, I love you, always.

Made in the USA
Coppell, TX
26 March 2020

17716349R00039